DISCOVERING THE DEAD SEA SCROLLS

Pacific Science Center
Seattle, Washington

Documentary Media

Seattle, Washington

Discovering The Dead Sea Scrolls

For information, write to Documentary Media LLC, 3250 41st Avenue S.W., Seattle, Washington 98116, or e-mail Books@docbooks.com.

First edition 2006

Printed in Canada

Managing editor: Petyr Beck, Ph.D.
Publisher: Barry Provorse
Interior book design: Paul Langland Design

ISBN 1-933245-02-6

Photographs by Clara Amit, Tsila Sagiv and Mariana Salzberger.
Photographs and texts used in this booklet were provided by
the Israel Antiquities Authority.
Cover photograph courtesy of the Israel Antiquities Authority

Table of Contents

Introduction

Welcome to Pacific Science Center and the exhibit *Discovering the Dead Sea Scrolls*. Curated by the Israel Antiquities Authority, this exhibit was developed by Pacific Science Center in Seattle, Washington, and Discovery Place in Charlotte, North Carolina, with the support of many generous donors. This commemorative guide has been designed to provide a lasting record of the ten scrolls that were exhibited in Seattle and a reminder of your experience at this rare and special exhibit.

Since the first discovery of these extraordinary documents in 1947, the world has been fascinated by the stories of history, faith, and culture that they present to us. Dating back to the period 250 BCE to 70 CE, these approximately 900 parchment and papyrus documents, written in three languages and found in thousands of fragments, allow us to look back into one of the most significant periods of history for the Western world.

This exhibition was created with the intent of sharing a story that has multiple layers of complexity and richness. As a science center we were particularly interested in demonstrating the role that modern science plays in helping us unravel the mysteries of their origin and content—and thereby helping us to understand some of the forces that have shaped civilization for the past 2,000 years. We encourage you to pursue your own further discovery in those areas that interest you, as we know that no exhibit can provide comprehensive coverage of any single topic.

I hope these beautiful scrolls and their translations will give you enjoyment and provide good memories of an extraordinary exhibit and story.

Bryce Seidl
President and CEO
Pacific Science Center

Map of modern-day Israel and surrounding regions. The Dead Sea scrolls were discovered in Qumran.

The Qumran Library

The writings recovered in the Judean Desert have presented us with a large number of Jewish documents dating from the third century BCE to 135 CE. The collection comprises varied documents, most of them of a distinctly religious orientation. The chief categories represented are Biblical, Apocryphal or pseudepigraphical, and Sectarian writings. The study of this original library has demonstrated that the boundaries between these categories are far from clear-cut. Joséf Milik developed a system for identifying scroll fragments. This system lists the cave number, the site, and the fragment number. For example, the siglum 4Q287 means that this scroll fragment was the 287th scroll manuscript associated with Cave 4 at Qumran.

Biblical Scrolls

The Biblical manuscripts include the earliest known copies of the Hebrew Bible.

Some 200 Biblical manuscripts containing texts from all the books of the Hebrew Bible (except for the book of Esther) were found in the caves of Qumran. Some of the books were more popular among the members of the sect, as attested by the numerous copies of those that were found, chiefly Psalms, Isaiah, and Deuteronomy. The Biblical texts display considerable similarity to the standard Masoretic text. This, however, is not always the rule; some of the texts follow the Septuagint.

The Biblical scrolls in general have provided many new readings that facilitate the reconstruction of the textual history of the Hebrew Bible. It is also significant that several manuscripts of the Bible, including the Leviticus Scroll, are inscribed not in the square script dominant at the time, but in the ancient paleo-Hebrew script.

Apocryphal Scrolls

A considerable number of Apocryphal and pseudepigraphic texts—formerly known only in later translations—are preserved at Qumran in their original Hebrew and Aramaic versions.

These writings, which were not included in the canonical Jewish scriptures, were preserved by different Christian churches and transmitted in Greek, Ethiopic, Syriac, Armenian, and other languages. A considerable number of Apocryphal books interpret and embellish what is concisely related in the Hebrew Bible.

Some of these are narrative texts closely related to Biblical documents, such as the Book of Jubilees and Enoch, whereas others are independent works. Apparently, some of these compositions were treated by the Qumran community as canonical and were studied by them.

Sectarian Scrolls

Sectarian writings, apparently written by and for the sect represented at Qumran and elsewhere in the Judean Desert, were practically unknown until their discovery among the Dead Sea Scrolls.

An exception is the Damascus Document, which lacked a definite identification before the other Dead Sea discoveries. The Sectarian writings reveal the beliefs and customs of a pious community, probably centered at Qumran, and include rules and ordinances, Biblical commentaries, apocalyptic visions, and liturgical works generally attributed to the last quarter of the second century BCE and onward.

Biblical commentaries (*pesharim*), such as the Habakkuk, Nahum, and Hosea, are common Sectarian writings. Commentaries cite scriptural verses assuming that the prophet was predicting events in the commentator's time period, and offer explanations accordingly.

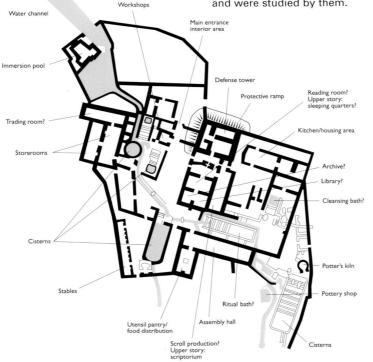

The Qumran Site

Water channel

Immersion pool

Trading room?

Storerooms

Cisterns

Stables

Workshops

Main entrance interior area

Defense tower

Protective ramp

Reading room? Upper story: sleeping quarters?

Kitchen/housing area

Archive?

Library?

Cleansing bath?

Potter's kiln

Pottery shop

Cisterns

Utensil pantry/ food distribution

Scroll production? Upper story: scriptorium

Assembly hall

Ritual bath?

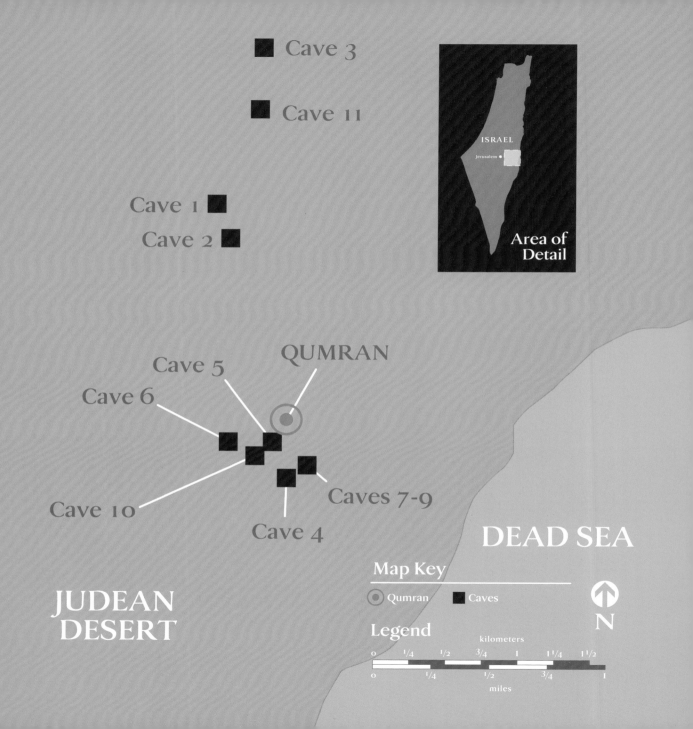

Cave 3

Cave 11

ISRAEL

Jerusalem

Area of Detail

Cave 1

Cave 2

Cave 5

QUMRAN

Cave 6

Cave 10

Caves 7-9

Cave 4

DEAD SEA

Map Key

Qumran   Caves

JUDEAN DESERT

Legend

N

kilometers

0   1/4   1/2   3/4   1   1 1/4   1 1/2

0   1/4   1/2   3/4   1

miles

11 cave sites where scrolls
were discovered

List of Scrolls Discovered Cave by Cave

Cave No.	Biblical Texts	Non-Biblical Texts
1	17	36
2	18	15
3	3	7
4	171	431
5	8	17
6	6	24
7	-	17
8	4	1
9	0	1
10	-	-
11	9	16

The individual texts were assembled
from more than 100,000 written
fragments found in the caves.

Scroll jar and lid
*Photograph courtesy of the
Israel Antiquities Authority*

Scriptorium bench reconstruction;
Rockefeller Museum, Jerusalem
*Photograph courtesy of the
Israel Antiquities Authority*

Genesis

A wide variety of writings were found in the 11 caves of Qumran, including some 200 biblical texts. Certain biblical books were more popular than others among the members of the sect, as attested by the many copies of these that were found: Psalms (30 copies), Isaiah (20 copies), Deuteronomy (25 copies), Exodus (14 copies), and Genesis (14 copies).

Some copies of the Book of Genesis had faded over the years, but the scroll displayed here is relatively well preserved and corresponds to Genesis 1:18-27. On the left margin of the scroll, the linen string that joined the various sheets of parchment can be discerned. The columns of the scroll are short, each with 11 lines, and the upper and lower borders of the text are clearly visible. There is a correction in the fifth line of the scroll, made by the scribe, who accidentally erased a letter and then added it above the line of writing, a common occurrence in the writings of Qumran.

The fragment exhibited here describes the act of creation that took place on the fifth day and ends with the creation of man on the sixth day. The writing is dated to the first half of the first century BCE.

4Q4
Plate 1071
11cm x 11cm
Photograph courtesy of the
Israel Antiquities Authority

1. the light from the darkness. And God saw that it was good.
   19: And there was evening

2. and there was morning, a fourth day. *20*: And God said,
   "Let the waters bring forth swarms of living creatures,

3. and let birds fly above the earth across the firmament of
   the heavens." *21*: So God created the great sea monsters

4. and every living creature that moves, with which the waters
   swarm, according to their kinds, and every winged bird
   according to its kind.

5. And God saw that it was good. *22*: And God blessed them,
   saying, "Be fruitful and multiply and fill the waters in the
   seas, and let birds multiply on the earth."

6. *23*: And there was evening and there was morning,
   a fifth day.

7. *24*: And God said, "Let the earth bring forth living creatures
   according to their kinds: cattle and creeping things and
   beasts of the earth according to their kinds." And it was so.

8. *25*: And God made the beasts of the earth according to their
   kinds and the cattle according to their kinds, and everything
   that creeps upon the ground according to its kind.

9. And God saw that it was good.

10. *26*: Then God said, "Let us make man in our image, after
    our likeness; and let them have dominion over the fish of
    the sea, and over the birds of the air, and over the cattle,
    and over all the earth, and over every creeping thing that
    creeps upon the earth."

11. *27*: So God created man in his own image, in the image of
    God he created him; male and female he created them.

האור ובﬠﬞין החושך וירא אלהים כﬠﬞן טוב ⁱ⁹ויהי ﬠﬞרﬞב ויהﬠﬞי	1]
vacatﬠﬞ ²⁰ויאמר אלהים יﬠﬞשרﬞצו המים שרץ	2]
עﬞול הארץ על פני רקיע השמים ﬠﬞ ²¹ויﬠﬞברﬞא אﬞלהים את התנינים	3]
הﬠﬞחיה הרמשת אשר שרצו המﬠﬞום למﬠﬞיניהם ואת כל	4]
אﬠﬞלﬞהים כﬠﬞיﬠﬞן טוב ﬠﬞ ²²ויברך אﬠﬞתם ﬠﬞ אלﬞהים לאמר פרו ורבו	5]
בﬠﬞארﬞץ ²³ויהי ﬠﬞרﬞב ﬠﬞ ויהﬠﬞיﬠﬞ בקר יום חמישי	6]
תﬠﬞוצﬞאﬠﬞ הﬠﬞארﬞץ נפש ﬠﬞ חיﬠﬞה ﬠﬞ למﬠﬞיﬠﬞנﬠﬞהﬠﬞ בהמה ורמש	7]²⁴
ﬠﬞחית הﬠﬞאﬠﬞרﬞץ למינﬠﬞה ואת הבהמה	8]²⁵
אלהים כי טוב vacat	9]
ויﬠﬞרﬞדו בדגת הים ובעוף השמים	10]²⁶
עﬞול הﬠﬞאﬠﬞרﬞץ ²⁷ויברא אלהים את האדם	11]

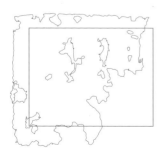

Transcription from *Discoveries in the
Judean Desert*, Volume XII. Translation
from the Revised Standard Version

Exodus

Approximately 14 copies of the Book of Exodus were found at Qumran. The scroll was written on the grain side of a carefully worked, relatively thick parchment. The surface of the scroll was cracked and damaged, as were those of most of the scrolls found in Cave 4.

The biblical scrolls from Qumran have contributed to the reconstruction of the textual history and transmission of the Bible, and the relationship between various versions. The scroll displayed here presents intriguing evidence for the existence of a version resembling the Septuagint.

Sometimes a word is spelled differently; at other times variations are preserved that differ from the standard Masoretic text. For example, in Line 5 of the upper right fragment, it is stated that the number of people of Israel that entered Egypt was 75, while the Masoretic version states 70. Furthermore, the order of appearance of the sons of Jacob is different in this scroll: Issachar, Zebulun, and Joseph, while in the Masoretic version the order is Issachar, Zebulun, and Benjamin.

The displayed scroll corresponds to the first chapters of the Book of Exodus, which relate the story of the descent of the sons of Joseph to Egypt and the process of becoming a people. It tells of the birth and deliverance of Moses, his maturity, and his first acquaintance with the God of Israel at the burning bush. The scroll is dated from the first half of the first century BCE to the first half of the first century CE.

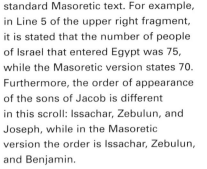

4Q13
Plate 659
23cm x 42.5cm
Photograph courtesy of the
Israel Antiquities Authority

1. *13* ... come to the people of Israel and say to them, `The God of your fathers has sent me to you,' and they ask me, `What

2. is his name?' what shall I say to them?" *14*: God said to Moses, "I AM WHO I AM."

3. And he said, "Say this to the people of Israel, `I AM has sent me to you.'"

4. *15*: God also said to Moses, "Say this to the people of Israel, `The LORD, the God of your fathers, the God of

5. Abraham, the God of Isaac, and the God of Jacob, has sent me to you': this is my name for ever, and thus I am to be remembered throughout all generations.

6. *16*: Go and gather the elders of Israel together, and say to them, `The LORD, the God of your fathers,

7. the God of Abraham, of Isaac, and of Jacob, has appeared to me, saying, "I have observed you and what has been done

8. to you in Egypt; *17*: and I promise that I will bring you up out of the affliction of Egypt, to the land of the Canaanites, the Hittites, the Amorites,

9. the Per'izzites, the Hivites, and the Jeb'usites, a land flowing with milk and honey."' *18*: And they will hearken to your voice; and you

10. and the elders of Israel shall go to the king of Egypt and say to him, `The•LORD, the God of the Hebrews, has met with us;

11. and now, we pray you, let us go a three days' journey into the wilderness, that we may sacrifice to the LORD our God.' *19*: I know that the king of Egypt will not

12. let you go unless compelled by a mighty hand. *20*: So I will stretch out my hand and smite Egypt

13. with all the wonders which I will do in it; after that he will let you go. *21*: And I will

1 ‏[בא אל בני ישראל ואמרתי א]ליהם אלוהי [אבותיכם שלחני אליכם ואמרו לי מה]

2 ‏[ש]מ[ו מה אומר א]ליהם ‏14‏ ויואמר אלוהים אל] מושה אהיה אשר אהיה ויואמר כה]

3 ‏תואמר אל בני ישראל אהיה שלחני אליכם ‏vacat‏ [

4 ‏ויואמר אלוהים עוד אל מושה כה תואמר אל בני ישראל יהוה אל]והי אבותיכם אלוהי ‏15

5 ‏אברהם אלוהי ישחק ואלוהי יעקוב שלחני אליכם זה שמי ל]עולם וזה זכרי לדור ודור]

6 ‏16‏ לך ואספתה את זקני בני ישרא]ל [ואמרת]ה אליהם יהוה אל[והי אבותיכם נראה אלי]

7 ‏אלוהי אברהם ואלוהי יש[חק ואלוהי] יעקוב לאמור פקוד [פקדתי אתכם ואת עשוי]

8 ‏לכם במצרים ‏17‏ ו] אמרה [אעלה אתכ]ם מעני מצרים אל[ארץ הכנעני החתי האמורי]

9 ‏הפרזי החוי והיבוסי והגרגשי] אל ארץ זבת חלב ודבוש ‏18‏ ישמעו לקולך ובאתה אתה]

10 ‏וזקני ‏בני‏ ישראל אל מלך מצרים] ואמרתם אליו יהוה אלוהי העברים נקרה עלינו]

11 ‏ועתה נלכה נא דרך שלושת ימי]ם במדבר ונזבחה ליהוה אל]והינו ‏19‏ ואני ידעתי כי לא]

12 ‏יתן אתכם מלך [מצרים ללכת כי אם ביד חזקה ‏20‏ ושלחתי את ידי והכיתי את מצרים]

13 ‏בכל נפלאותי [אשר אעשה] בקרבו ואחרי כן ישלח אתכם ‏21‏ וכן]

Transcription from *Discoveries in the Judean Desert*, Volume XII. Translation from the Revised Standard Version

Isaiah

Apart from the complete scroll (66 chapters) of the Book of Isaiah from Cave 1, approximately 18 additional copies of this book were recovered. The numerous copies apparently indicate the great popularity of the Book of Isaiah among the members of the sect. This special status is also seen in the sectarian manuscripts, which contain many quotations from the Book of Isaiah.

The fragments exhibited here belong to the last section of the book, known among scholars as "Second Isaiah." In Chapter 54 the prophet compares Jerusalem to a barren widow who will be redeemed of her shame. Later on in the chapter, God testifies that he will renew the contract between himself and Israel and will never break it, which was similar to the contract he made with Noah after the flood. Many prophets have compared Zion to a woman, but none have made use of the many family and social aspects of women as extensively as Isaiah did to illustrate his messages.

Parts of nine columns were preserved from the original 12, each column containing some 24 lines. The scroll was found in Cave 4 and is dated to the first century CE.

4Q58
Plate 236
19cm x 46.5cm
Photograph courtesy of the
Israel Antiquities Authority

16.

17. *9*: And they made his grave with the wicked and with a rich man in his death, although

18. he had done no violence, and there was no deceit in his mouth. *10*: Yet it was the will of the LORD

19. to bruise him; he has put him to grief; when he makes himself an offering for sin, he shall see his offspring, he shall prolong his days; the will of the LORD shall prosper in his hand;

20. *11*: he shall see the fruit of the travail of his soul and be satisfied; by his knowledge shall the righteous one, my servant, make many to be accounted righteous; and

21. he shall bear their iniquities. *12*: Therefore I will divide him a portion with the great, and he shall divide the spoil with the strong; because he poured out his soul to death,

22. and was numbered with the transgressors; yet he bore the sin of many, and made intercession for the transgressors.

23. *1*: "Sing, O barren one, who did not bear; break forth into singing and cry aloud, you who have not been in travail! For the children of the desolate one will be more than the children

24. of her that is married, says the LORD. 2: Enlarge the place of your tent, and let the curtains of your habitations be stretched out; hold not back, lengthen your cords and strengthen your stakes.

[	][	]	16
[	מפש]ע עמי נגע למו ⁹ ויתן את]	]	17
[	חמ]ס עשה ולא מרמה בפיהו ¹⁰ ויהוה חפץ]	]	18
[ד]כאו החלי אם תשם אשם נ[פשו י]ראה זרע והאריך ימים וחפץ יהוה בידו]			19
יצלח ¹¹ מעמל נפשו יראה יו[ר]ושבע בדעתו יצדיק צדיק עבדי לר]בים ועונתם]			20
הוא יסבול ¹² לכ]ן אחלק לו ברבים ואת עצמים יחלק שלל תחת אשר הערה למות]			21
[	vacat	נפשו ואת פשעים נמנה והוא חטאי רבים נשא ולפשעיה[ם יפגיע		22
[	רני עקרה ולא ילדה פצחי רנה וצהלי לא חלה כי רבים בנ]י	⁵⁴:¹	23
בעולה אמר יהוה ² הרחיבי מקום אהלך ויריעות משכנותיך [יטו אל תחשכי]			24

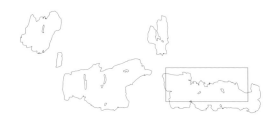

Transcription from *Discoveries in the Judean Desert*, Volume XII. Translation from the Revised Standard Version

Ezekiel

This scroll was discovered in Cave 4 and is composed of four fragments, two of which are exhibited here. These two fragments preserve the first columns of the scroll containing the text of Ezekiel 10:6–11:11. It is worth noting that the text in this scroll is identical to the standard version of the Bible, apart from six small differences in spelling. After studying the arrangement of the text, scholars believe that the entire scroll was composed of 47 columns, each column containing 42 lines. The scroll is dated on paleographic grounds to the first half of the first century BCE.

Ezekiel was deported to Babylon at the time of the exile of Jehoiachin, in 598 BCE, and there he prophesied to his fellow exiles. There is a significant difference in the contents of his prophesies from before the destruction of Jerusalem and after. Up until the destruction, Ezekiel admonished the exiles for their sins, which, in his words, had brought about their exile and enslavement. Following the destruction, Ezekiel's visions were now of redemption and the return of the exiles to the Land of Israel.

In the fragment exhibited here, Ezekiel describes his vision of the divine chariot and the destruction of Jerusalem.

4Q73
Plate 1112
19cm x 17cm
Photograph courtesy of the
Israel Antiquities Authority

1. *17*: When they stood still, these stood still, and when they mounted up, these mounted up with them; for the spirit of the living creatures was in them. *18*: Then the
2. glory of the LORD went forth from the threshold of the house, and stood over the cherubim. *19*: And the cherubim lifted up
3. their wings and mounted up from the earth in my sight as they went forth, with the wheels beside them;
4. and they stood at the door of the east gate of the house of the LORD; and the glory of the God of Israel was over them.
5. *20*: These were the living creatures that I saw underneath the God of Israel by the river Chebar; and I knew that they were cherubim.
6. *21*: Each had four faces, and each four wings, and underneath their wings the semblance of human hands.
7. *22*: And as for the likeness of their faces, they were the very faces whose appearance I had seen by the river Chebar.
8. They went every one straight forward. *1*: The Spirit lifted me up, and brought me to the east gate
9. of the house of the LORD, which faces east. And behold, at the door of the gateway
10. there were twenty-five men; and I saw among them Ja-azani'ah the son of Azzur, and Pelati'ah the son of Benai'ah, princes of the people.
11. *Blank*
12. *2*: And he said to me, "Son of man, these are the men who devise iniquity and who give wicked counsel in this city;
13. *3*: who say, `The time is not near to build houses; this city is the caldron, and we are the flesh.'
14. *4*: Therefore prophesy against them, prophesy, O son of man." *5*: And the Spirit of the LORD fell upon me,
15. and he said to me, "Say, Thus says the LORD: So you think, O house of Israel; for I know the things that come into your mind.
16. *6*: You have multiplied your slain in this city, and have filled its streets with the slain.
17. *7*: Therefore thus says the Lord GOD: Your slain whom you have laid in the midst of it, they are the flesh, and this city is the caldron; but you shall be brought forth out of the midst of it.
18. *8*: You have feared the sword; and I will bring the sword upon you, says the Lord GOD.
19. *9*: And I will bring you forth out of the midst of it, and give you into the hands of foreigners, and execute judgments upon you.
20. *10*: You shall fall by the sword; I will judge you at the border of Israel; and you shall know that I am the LORD.
21. *11*: This city shall not be your caldron, nor shall you be the flesh in the midst of it; I will judge you at the border of Israel;

[	¹⁷בעמדם יעמדו וברומם ירומו אותם כ[ן	1
[	[כב]וד יהוה מעל מפתן הבית ויעמד על הכרובים ¹⁹ו[ן]ישאו	2
[	[כנפי]הם וירומו מן הארץ לעיני בצאתם והאופנים	3
[	יהוה הקדמוני וכבוד אל[ו]הי ישראל ע[ל]יהם]	4
[	[ראיתי תחת אלהי ישראל בנהר כבר]	5
[	פנ[י]ם לאחד וארבעה כנפים לא[ח]חד]	6
[	פניהם המה הפנים אשר[²²]	7
[	אי[ש] אל עבר פניו ילכו ¹¹⁺¹ ותש[א]	8
[	[הקדמוני הפונה קדמה]	9
[	וארא]ה בתוכם את יאזני]ה]	10
[	] VACAT [ ]	11
[	ו ה[ח]שבים און והיעצים ²]	12
[	[בתים היא הסיר]	13
[	[ותפל עלי רוח יהוה ⁵]	14
[	[ישראל ומעלות]	15
[	הז[ו]את ומלאתם חו[צ]תיה]	16
[	[שמתם בתוכה] ⁷]	17
[	[חרב יראתם] ⁸]	18
[	[והוצאתי אתכ]ם מתוכה] ⁹	19
[	[בחרב] תפלו ע[ל ¹⁰]	20
[	[הי]א[¹¹]	21

Transcription from *Discoveries in the Judean Desert*, Volume XV. Translation from the Revised Standard Version

Psalms

The Psalms scroll, found in Cave 11 in 1956, is one of the longer texts from Qumran. The scroll contains 28 incomplete columns of text, eight of which are displayed here. It is clear that six to seven lines are missing from the bottom of each column. In this scroll the tetragrammaton (the four-letter divine name), inscribed in the paleo-Hebrew script, is clearly discernible. On paleographic grounds, the manuscript is dated between 30 and 50 CE.

This impressive scroll is a liturgical collection of psalms and hymns, comprising parts of 41 biblical psalms in non-canonical sequence and with variations in detail. It also contains apocryphal psalms (previously unknown hymns dealing with the future), as well as a prose passage about the psalms composed by King David: ". . . And the total was 4,050. All these he composed through prophecy, which was given him from before the Most High" (11QPsa 27:10-11).

The displayed fragment is part of Psalm 119, the longest of the psalms, containing 176 verses. The psalm is composed of 22 stanzas, corresponding to the number of letters in the Hebrew alphabet. Each stanza begins with a different letter, in alphabetical order, and the eight lines in every stanza begin with the same letter. The division of the psalm into stanzas is visually evident. The speaker praises the Torah and hopes to overcome his enemies by reciting and studying the Torah.

11Q5
Plate 979
17.5cm x 105cm
Photograph courtesy of the
Israel Antiquities Authority

1. *82*: My eyes fail with watching for thy promise; I ask, "When wilt thou comfort me?"

2. *83*: For I have become like a wineskin in the smoke, yet I have not forgotten thy statutes.

3. *84*: How long must thy servant endure? When wilt thou judge those who persecute me?

4. *85*: Godless men have dug pitfalls for me, men who do not conform to thy law.

5. *86*: All thy commandments are sure; they persecute me with falsehood; help me!

6. *87*: They have almost made an end of me on earth; but I have not forsaken thy precepts.

7. *88*: In thy steadfast love spare my life, that I may keep the testimonies of thy mouth.

8. *89*: For ever, O LORD, thy word is firmly fixed in the heavens.

9. *90*: Thy faithfulness endures to all generations; thou hast established the earth, and it stands fast.

10. *91*: By thy appointment they stand this day; for all things are thy servants.

11. *92*: If thy law had not been my delight, I should have perished in my affliction.

12. *93*: I will never forget thy precepts; for by them thou hast given me life.

13. *94*: I am thine, save me; for I have sought thy precepts.

14. *95*: The wicked lie in wait to destroy me; but I consider thy testimonies.

15. *96*: I have seen a limit to all perfection, but thy commandment is exceedingly broad.

1 ‏כלתה עיני לאמרתכה לאמר מתי תנחמני‏⁸²
2 ‏כי עשיתני כנאוד בקיטור חסדכה לוא שכחתי‏⁸³
3 ‏כמה ימי עבדכה מתי תעשה ברודפי משפט‏⁸⁴
4 ‏כרו לי זידים שחת אשר לוא כתורתכה‏⁸⁵
5 ‏כול מצוותיכה אמונה שקר רדפוני עזרני‏⁸⁶
6 ‏כמעט כלוני מארץ ואני לוא עזבתי פקודיכה‏⁸⁷
7 ‏כחסדכה חונני ואשמורה עדוות פיכה‏⁸⁸

8 ‏לעולם‏⁸⁹ יהוה דברכה נצב בשמים
9 ‏לדור ודור אמונתכה כוננתה ארץ ותעמד‏⁹⁰
10 ‏למשפטיכה עמדו היום כי הכול עבדיכה‏⁹¹
11 ‏לולי תורתכה שעשועי אז אבדתי בעווני‏⁹²
12 ‏לעולם לוא אשכח פקודיכה כי במה חייתני‏⁹³
13 ‏לכה אני הושיעני כי פקודיכה דרשתי‏⁹⁴
14 ‏לי קוו רשעים לאבדני עדוותיכה אתבונן‏⁹⁵
15 ‏לכול תכלה ראיתי קץ רחבה מצותכ[ ] מואדה‏⁹⁶

Transcription from *Discoveries in the Judean Desert*, Volume IV. Translation from the Revised Standard Version

Community Rule *(Serekh ha-Yahad)*

The "Community Rule" *(Serekh ha-Yahad)* comprises a set of rules according to which the members of the Judean Desert sect conducted their lives. Most scholars identify this sect with the Essenes, although the name Essene is not mentioned in any of the scrolls. The members of the sect called themselves "men of the community," "council of the community," and the "sons of light." This scroll is the book of laws and contains instructions and regulations concerning the everyday conduct of the community, including matters of religion, punishment, and initiation.

The laws were written in Hebrew and there are at least 12 copies, indicative of the importance of this composition to the members of the sect. A complete copy was recovered in Cave 1 at Qumran in 1947.

The six preserved fragments of Scroll 4Q260 that are displayed here correspond with the final columns of the copy found in Cave 1, and thus the two versions can be completed and compared. In the fragment displayed here, members of the sect are obligated to refrain from falsehood and deceit, and follow the way of goodness and righteousness.

The scroll was found in Cave 4 and is dated to the second half of the first century BCE.

4Q260
Plate 366
7.6cm x 49cm
Photograph courtesy of the
Israel Antiquities Authority

1. [I will have no com]passion on any who deviate from the way. I will have no pity on the straightforward(?) till they have mended

2. their w[a]ys. And I will not keep Belial in my heart. And there shall not be heard in my mouth

3. foolish things and wicked lying, [and de]ceptions and false-hoods shall not be found on my lips.

4. And the fruit of holiness (shall be) on my tongue, vacat and abominations shall not be found

5. thereon. In songs of thanksgi[ving I will o]pe[n] vacat my mouth [and] my tongue shall rec[ount] the righteous acts of God

6. contin[uously, as well as the faithlessness] of men, un[til] their sinful rebellion [comes to an e]nd. [Vanities]

7. [I will cause to cease from my lips, impurities and perversions] from [the knowledge of my heart With wise counsel]

1   אר[חם] ²¹ על כול סוררי דרך לוא אנחם בנכוחים עד תום

2   ד[רכ]ם ובליעל לוא אשמור בלבבי ולוא ישמע בפי

3   נבלות וכחש עוון [ומ]רמות וכזבים לוא ימצאו בשפתי ²²

4   ופרי קודש בלשוני vacat ושקוצים ²³ לוא ימצאו

5   בה בהוד[ות אפ]תח [vacat פי ו]צדקות אל תס[פר]

6   לשוני תמ[יד ומעל] אנשים עד ת[ום ²⁴ פשעם] רקים

7   [אשבית משפתי נדות ונפתלות] מ[דעת לבי בעצת תושיה]

Transcription and translation from *Discoveries in the Judean Desert*, Volume XXVI.

Hosea Commentary

The Qumran manuscripts have provided us with much information on the period prior to the destruction of the Second Temple. We learn of the methods of Bible instruction and the use in that period of ideas from the Bible, of the language and style of writing, and of the sectarians' reliance on the Bible and their unique style of biblical commentary—the *pesher* method.

Pesher (commentary) is characteristic of the Qumran sect. The sectarian writers quoted biblical texts, and after each quote attempted to interpret how the words of the Bible had been realized in contemporary events according to the world view of the sect. The members of the sect viewed the books of the Bible as writings containing secrets and hidden meanings that revealed the future, which they, as the only true believers, were imbued with the power to understand.

This commentary of Hosea includes quotes from Chapter 2:8-14 and their interpretation. The failing relationship between the husband and wife is used as a metaphor for the relations between God and the people of Israel. The expected punishment for the sinful wife is hunger and disgrace, an allegory for the punishment awaiting those within Israel who have sinned.

The commentary was found in Cave 4 and is dated to the first century BCE.

4Q166
Plate 675
17cm x 16.5cm
Photograph courtesy of the
Israel Antiquities Authority

1. [2:10 she does not know that] it was I who gave her
   wheat, [wine]
2. [and oil.] I increased [the silver] and the gold (which) they used
   [for Ba'al.. Its interpretation:]
3. they at[e and] became replete and forgot the God of
   [justice, and]
4. cast behind their back [all] his precepts which he had sent to
   them [through]
5. his servants, the prophets. But they listened to those who
   misdirected them and they acclaimed them
6. and feared them in their blindness like gods. *Blank*
7. *Blank*
8. *2: 11-12* Because of this I will collect back my wheat in its time
   and my wine [in its season]
9. I will reclaim my wool and my flax so that she cannot cover
   [her nakedness.]
10. Now I will uncover her disgrace in the sight of [her] love[rs
    and] no [one]
11. will free her from my hand. *Blank*
12. its interpretation: he has punished them with hunger and with
    nakedness so they will be sham[e]
13. and disgrace in the eyes of the nations on whom they relied.
    But they
14. will not save them from their sufferings. *2:13* I will make an
    end to her joys,
15. her fea[st, her new] moon and her Sabbath and all her
    celebrations. Its interpretation:
16. they fix [all cele]brations in agreement with the celebrations of
    the nations, but a[ll]
17. [joy] will be changed into mourning for them. *2:14* I will
    devastate [her vine]
18. [and her fig tree] about which she said: they are their gifts
    for me [which]
19. my [lovers gave me;] I will turn them into thickets and the
    [wild be]asts will eat them.

[לוא ידעה כיא] אנוכי נתתי לה הדגן [והתירוש]	1
[והיצהר וכסף] הרביתי וזהב עשו [לבעל פשרו]	2
אשר אכלו וי[שבעו וישכחו את אל המש]פט ואת כול]	3
מצוותיו השליכו אחרי גום אשר שלח אליהם [בפי]	4
עבדיו הנביאים ולמתעיהם שמעו ויכבדום	5
וכאלים יפחדו מהם בעורונם vacat	6
vacat	7
לכן אשוב ולקחתי דגני בעתו ותירושי [במעדו]	8
והצלתי צמרי ופושתי מלכסות את [ערותה]	9
ועתה אגלה את נבלותה לעיני מאה]ביה ואיש]	10
לוא יצילנה מידי vacat	11
פשרו אשר הכם ברעב ובערום להיות לקלו[ן]	12
וחרפה לעיני הגואים אשר נשענו עליהם והמה	13
לוא יושיעום מצרותיהם והשבתי כול משושה	14
ח[גה חד]שה ושבתה וכול מועדיה פשרו אשר	15
[כול המו]עדות יוליכו במועדי הגואים vacat וכ[ול]	16
[שמחה] נהפכה להם לאבל והשמותי [גפנה]	17
[ותאנתה] אשר אמרה אתנם הם לי [אשר נתנו]	18
[לי מאהבי] ושמתים ליער ואכלתם חית השדה]	19

Transcription and translation from
The Dead Sea Scrolls, Study Edition, by
F.G. Martinez and E.J.C. Tigchelaar

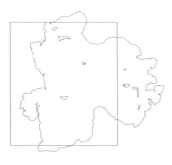

Calendrical Document

Fragments of 20 compositions dealing with the calendar and the holy seasons were discovered at Qumran. These important texts set the Qumran community apart from the rest of Judaism in the crucial matter of reckoning time.

The calendars combine one natural and two religious cycles. The natural cycle is the solar year. In this the Qumran sect was different from mainstream Judaism, whose 354-day calendar—still in use today—was established on the lunar month.

Into this 364-day solar calendar they incorporated the 24 priestly courses of 1 Chronicles 24:7-19. Each week was named after the priestly family responsible for the service of the temple. Although the Qumran sect had denounced the temple and its method of worship, they viewed this state of affairs as temporary, and they prepared for the time when they would again be able to worship God in Jerusalem.

The second religious cycle charted the festivals and holy days. The use of different calendars engendered a sharp separation between the two groups and a different way of life, since each group would have celebrated festivals and holy days at different times. The scroll fragment in this display enumerates the holy seasons in the same order as other scrolls: Passover first, followed by the festival of *se'orim*, probably the "waving of the first sheaf." This scroll was found in Cave 4 and is dated to the end of the first century BCE.

4Q325
Plate 226/1
6cm x 10.6cm
Photograph courtesy of the
Israel Antiquities Authority

1. [...the Passover is on the fourteenth of the month on the thi]rd [day.] On the eighteenth of the month is the Sabbath o[f Jehoiarib. Passover ends]

2. [on the third day] in the evening. On the twenty-fifth of the month is the Sabbath of Jedaiah, its responsibility [includes]

3. the Barley [Festiva]l on the twenty-sixth of the month, on the day after the Sabbath. The beginning of the se[cond month is]

4. [on the si]xth [day of the week] of Jedaiah. On the second of the month is the Sabbath of Harim. On the ninth of the month is the Sabbath of

5. [Seorim.] On the sixteenth of the month is the Sabbath of Malchijah. On the twenty-third of the [month]

1 [הפסח יום שלי]שי בשמונה עשר בו שבת ע[ל יויריב

2 [ ] בערב בעשרים וחמשה בו שבת על ידעיה ועלו]

3 [מוע]ד שעורים בעשרים וששה בו אחר שבת רוש החודש הש[ני]

4 [בששה בשבת] על ידעיה בשנים בו שבת חרים בתשעה בו שבת

5 [שעורים] בששה עשר בו שבת מלכיה בעשרים ושלושה בו [

Transcription and translation from
The Dead Sea Scrolls: A New Translation,
by Michael Wise, Martin Abegg Jr.,
and Edward Cook

Book of War *(Sefer ha-Milhamah)*

The war between the forces of righteousness and the forces of evil is the apocalyptic vision of the war at the End of Days, wherein the sons of light—that is, the members of the sect—will conquer the entire world in stages and completely defeat the sons of darkness. The scroll on display relates the events that will occur at the end of the war. At the center of these events is a figure called "the Prince of the Congregation," who will play a key role.

Although several copies of the "War Rule" were found in the caves, this particular part of the composition appears in only one other scroll (11Q14 from Cave 11). It is, therefore, assumed to be connected to the more complete War Rule manuscript that was recovered in Cave 1. However, since the relationship between the two compositions is not sufficiently clear, this exhibit from Cave 4 is called the "Book of War" *(Sefer ha-Milhamah).*

The present arrangement of the scroll is only tentative, but the fragments exhibited here appear to have been originally part of a scroll with six columns, each of which had approximately 13 lines. The fragment on display refers to the vision related in Isaiah 10:34–11:1 of the Branch of David, identified by the writer with the Prince of the Congregation. The event described is the trial of the king of the Kittim (Rome) by the Great Priest and the Prince of the Congregation at the end of the war, in order to purge the land from the Kittim (Roman) sinners. The scroll was found in Cave 4 and is dated to the end of the first century BCE.

4Q285
Plate 301
9cm x 35.5cm
Photograph courtesy of the Israel Antiquities Authority

1. [As it is written in the book of] Isaiah the prophet:
   "Cut down shall be
2. [the thickets of the forest with an axe, and the Lebanon by a majestic one shall f]all. And there shall come forth a shoot from the stump of Jesse,
3. [and out of his roots a sapling will grow".] the Branch of David, and they will enter into judgement with
4. [ ] and the Prince of the Congregation, the Bran[ch of David,] shall put him to death
5. [by stroke(?)]s and wounds(?). And a priest [of renown(?)] will command
6. [the s]lai[n] of Kittim[ ] [ ]

כאשר כתוב בספר ‎] ישעיהו הנביא ונוקפ[ו‎]	1
‎]סבכי היער בברזל ולבנון באדיר י[פול ויצא חוטר מגזע ישי	2
‎]ונצר משורשיו יפרה צמח דויד ונשפטו את	3
‎]והמיתו נשיא העדה צמ[ח‎]	4
‎]דויד בנגעי[ם ובמחוללות וצוה כוהן	5
‎]השם ח[ללי] כתיים ‎] [ל[‎]	6

Transcription and translation from *Discoveries in the Judean Desert*, Volume XXXVI

Pseudo-Ezekiel

The term pseudepigraphy applies to a composition that is falsely attributed to an ancient author. Pseudo-Ezekiel is a reworking of Chapters 37 to 43 of the biblical Book of Ezekiel.

The present composition describes a dialogue between God and the prophet, with God helping the prophet to understand the visions revealed to him. The first column, much of which has broken away, relates to the vision of the dry bones that appears in Ezekiel 37:1-14. The second column describes the extra-biblical vision revealed to Ezekiel concerning the desolation of the land and the events that will occur in Egypt, and their connection with the return of the people of Israel to their land. The third column deals with the vision of the impending fall of Babylon.

Some scholars suggest that evidence for the date of this composition can be found in the name of the enemy of Israel, Belial, and his connection with the city of Memphis in Egypt, which is called Maf in this manuscript. However, there are other possible interpretations, and the identification of the figures and events in this scroll remain enigmatic. The fragment displayed here was found in Cave 4, and is dated on paleographic grounds to the first century BCE.

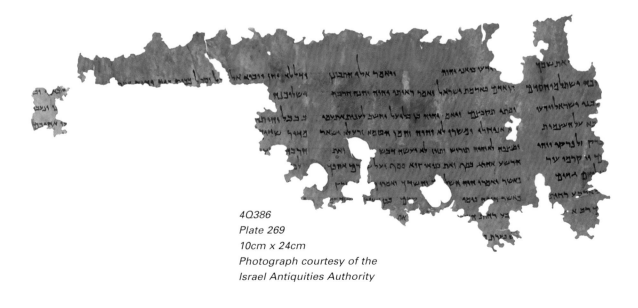

4Q386
Plate 269
10cm x 24cm
Photograph courtesy of the
Israel Antiquities Authority

1. [lan]d and they shall know that I am the Lord" *Blank* And he said to me, "Look
2. O son of man, at the land of Israel". And I said, "I have seen, Lord, and behold it lies waste,
3. And when will you gather them together?" And the Lord said, "A son of Belial will scheme to oppress my people
4. But I will not allow him; and his kin will not survive, nor will there be left from the impure one any seed;
5. And from the caperbush there shall be no wine, nor will a hornet make any honey. [ ] And the
6. Wicked one I will slay at Memphis but my children I will bring forth from Memphis, and their rem[na]nt I shall return.
7. As they shall say "peace and tranquility have come", and they shall say "the land sh[a]ll be
8. As it was in the days of [ ] old". Then I will raise upo[n] them wra[th]
9. From the [fo]ur corners of the heaven[s] [ ] [ ]
10. [like] a burning [fi]re as [ ]

1 ‏[ואר]ץ וידעו כי אני יהוה VACAT ויאמר אלי התבונן
2 ‏בן אדם באדמת ישראל ואמר ראיתי יהוה והנה חרבה
3 ‏ומתי תקבצם ויאמר יהוה בן בליעל יחשב לענות את עמי
4 ‏ולא אניח לו ומשרו לא יהיה והמן הטמא זרע לא ישאר
5 ‏ומנצפה לא יהיה תירוש ותזיז לא יעשה דבש [ ] ואת
6 ‏הרשע אהרג במף ואת בני אוציא ממף ועל שא]ר[ם אהפך
7 ‏כאשר יאמרו היה השל[ו]ם והשדך ואמרו תהי]ה[הארץ
8 ‏כאשר היתה בימי [ ] קדם בכן אעיר ע[ל]יהם חמ]ה[
9 ‏מ[אר]בע רחות השמי]ם [ל]ו [ ] את   [
10 ‏[כא]ש בערת כ[[

Transcription and translation from
Discoveries in the Judean Desert,
Volume XXX

Linen scroll cloth, found in Cave 7
Photograph courtesy of the
Israel Antiquities Authority

Major Sponsors and Donors

The Seattle exhibition of *Discovering the Dead Sea Scrolls* was made possible through generous private and public support. We are most grateful for the vision, leadership, and generosity of:*

$100,000 and above

Ginger and Barry Ackerley
  Presenting Sponsor
  Education and Public Programs
Martin Selig
  Presenting Sponsor
  Discovering the Dead Sea
    Scrolls Exhibit

Washington State Department of
  Community, Trade &
  Economic Development
King County
Mayor's Office of Arts & Cultural
  Affairs, City of Seattle
Federal Council on the Arts and
  the Humanities

$50,000-$99,999

Anonymous
Hydrogen
Gaye and Jim Pigott

$25,000-$49,999

Becky and Jack Benaroya
Herb and Shirley Bridge
Costco, Inc.
Joshua Green Foundation
Peter and Peggy Horvitz
Kibble & Prentice
Charles Simonyi Fund for Arts
  and Sciences

$15,000-$24,999

Green Diamond Resource Company
Northern Trust
Gwenn and Dean Polik
U.S. Bank

$10,000-$14,999

Ellsworth and Nancy Alvord
Doug Beighle and Kathleen Pierce
Wanda and James P. Cowles
Jim and Diana Judson
Juniper Foundation
Rosetta Inpharmatics,
  a Merck & Co. research subsidiary
Stroum Family Foundation

$5,000-$9,999—Gold Discovery

Anonymous (2)
James W. and Dee Claypool
David and Dorothy Fluke
Keith Grinstein and Claire Angel
Martha and Colin Moseley
Judy Pigott
Althea Stroum
Symetra Financial

as of June 30, 2006

Scrollery at the Rockefeller
Museum, Jerusalem
*Photograph courtesy of the
Israel Antiquities Authority*